Everyone Needs Someone

POEMS OF LOVE AND FRIENDSHIP

Helen Steiner Rice

Guideposts
Carmel, New York 10512

Contents

"Dear Friends"

We all need words to live by,
To inspire us and guide us,
Words to give us courage
When the trials of life betide us—
And the words that never fail us
Are the words of God above,
Words of comfort and of courage
Filled with wisdom and with love—
They are ageless and enduring
They have lived through generations,
There's no question left unanswered
In Our Father's revelations—
And in this ever-changing world
God's words remain unchanged,
For though through countless ages
They've been often re-arranged,
The *truth* shines through all changes
Just as *bright today* as when
Our Father made the *Universe*
And breathed His Life in men—
And the words of inspiration
That I write for you today
Are just the old enduring truths
Said in a rhythmic way—
And if my "borrowed words of truth"
In some way touch your heart,
Then I am deeply thankful
To have had a little part
In sharing these *God-given lines*,
And I hope you'll share them, too,
With family, friends and loved ones
And all those dear to you.

Helen Steiner Rice

Everyone Needs Someone

People need people and friends need friends,
And we all need love for a full life depends
Not on vast riches or great acclaim,
Not on success or on worldly fame,
But just in knowing that someone cares
And holds us close in their thoughts and prayers—
For only the knowledge that we're understood
Makes everyday living feel *wonderfully good*,
And we rob ourselves of life's greatest need
When we "lock up our hearts" and fail to heed
The outstretched hand reaching to find
A kindred spirit whose heart and mind
Are lonely and longing to somehow share
Our joys and sorrows and to make us aware
That life's completeness and richness depends
On the things we share with our loved ones and friends.

The Soul of Man

Every man has a deep heart need
    that cannot be filled with doctrine or creed,
For the soul of man knows nothing more
    than just that he is longing for
A haven that is safe and sure,
    a fortress where he feels secure,
An island in this sea of strife
    away from all the storms of life . . .
Oh, God of love, who sees us all,
    You are SO GREAT! We are so small!
Hear man's universal prayer
    crying to You in despair—
"Save my soul and grant me peace,
    let my restless murmurings cease,
God of love—Forgive! Forgive!
    teach me how to TRULY LIVE,
Ask me not my race or creed,
    just take me in my hour of need,
And let me know You love me, too,
    and that I am A PART OF YOU" . . .
And someday may man realize
    that all the earth, the seas and skies
Belong to God who made us all,
    the rich, the poor, the great, the small,
And in the Father's Holy Sight
    no man is yellow, black or white,
And PEACE ON EARTH cannot be found
    until we MEET ON COMMON GROUND
And every man becomes a BROTHER
    who worships God and loves each other.

We All Need Somebody

And SOMEBODY like YOU
    can "turn the trick,"
For our lives are empty
    and our world is "sick" . . .
We have lost our morals
    and our principles, too,
And with no purpose in life
    we are lonely and blue . . .
We need SOMEBODY very much
    who has a warm and friendly touch
To make us suddenly aware
    that there are those WHO REALLY CARE!

Everybody Everywhere Needs Somebody Sometime

Everybody, everywhere,
    no matter what his station,
Has moments of deep loneliness
    and quiet desperation,
For this lost and lonely feeling
    is inherent in mankind—
It is just the *Spirit speaking*
    as God tries again to find

An opening in the "worldly wall"
　　man builds against God's touch,
For he feels so self-sufficient
　　that he does not need God much,
So he vainly goes on struggling
　　to find some explanation
For these disturbing, lonely moods
　　of inner isolation . . .
But the answer keeps eluding him
　　for in his selfish, finite mind
He does not even recognize
　　that he cannot ever find
The reason for life's emptiness
　　unless he learns to share
The problems and the burdens
　　that surround him everywhere—
But when his eyes are opened
　　and he looks with love at others
He begins to see not *strangers*
　　but understanding brothers . . .
So open up your hardened hearts
　　and let God enter in—
He only wants to help you
　　a *new life to begin* . . .
And *every day's a good day*
　　to lose yourself in others
And *any time a good time*
　　to see mankind as brothers,
And this can only happen
　　when you realize it's true
That *everyone needs someone*
　　and that *someone is you!*

The Magic of Love

Love is like *magic.*
And it always will be,
For love still remains
Life's sweet mystery!

Love works in ways
That are wondrous and strange
And there's *nothing in life*
That *love cannot change!*

Love can transform
The most commonplace
Into beauty and splendor
And sweetness and grace!

Love is unselfish,
Understanding and kind,
For it sees with its *heart*
And not with its mind!

Love is the answer
That everyone seeks—
Love is the language
That every heart speaks—

Love can't be bought,
It is priceless and free,
Love like pure *magic*
Is a *sweet mystery!*

Love One Another for Love Is of God

Every couple should remember
  that what the world calls love
Is not something man invented,
  but it comes from God above . . .
And love can be neglected
  and oftentimes abused,
Perverted and distorted,
  misguided and misused,
Or it can be developed
  by living every day
Near to God, *Our Father*,
  and following in *His Way* . . .
For God alone can teach you
  the meaning of true love,
And He can help establish
  the life you're dreaming of
In which you live together
  in happiness and peace,
Enjoying married blessings
  that day by day increase . . .
For love that is immortal
  has its source in God above,
And the love you give each other
  is founded on His love . . .
And though upon *your wedding day*
  it seems *yours* and *yours alone,*
If you but ask, God takes *your love*
  and blends it with *His Own.*

When Two People Marry

Your hearts are filled with happiness
    so great and overflowing,
You cannot comprehend it
    for it's far beyond all knowing
How any heart could hold such joy
    or feel the fullness of
The wonder and the glory
    and the ecstasy of love—
You wish that you could capture it
    and never let it go
So you might walk forever
    in its radiant magic glow . . .
But love in all its ecstasy
    is such a fragile thing,
Like gossamer in cloudless skies
    or a hummingbird's small wing,
But love that lasts *forever*
    must be made of something strong,
The kind of strength that's gathered
    when the heart can hear no song—
When the "sunshine" of your wedding day
    runs into "stormy weather"
And hand in hand you brave the gale
    and climb steep hills together,
And clinging to each other
    while the thunder rolls above
You seek divine protection
    in *Faith* and *Hope* and *Love* . . .
For *"days of wine and roses"*
    never make love's dream come true,
It takes sacrifice and teardrops,
    and problems shared by two,
To give true love its *beauty*,
    its *grandeur* and its *fineness*
And to mold an "earthly ecstasy"
    into *Heavenly divineness*.

What Is Marriage?

Marriage is the union of two people in love,
And love is sheer magic for it's woven of
Gossamer dreams, enchantingly real,
That people in love are privileged to feel—
But the "exquisite ecstasy" that captures the heart
Of two people in love is just a small part
Of the beauty and wonder and *miracle* of
The growth and fulfillment and evolvement of love—
For only long years of living together
And sharing and caring in all kinds of weather
Both pleasure and pain, the glad and the sad,
Teardrops and laughter, the good and the bad,
Can add new dimensions and lift love above
The rapturous ecstasies of "falling in love"—
For ecstasy passes but it is replaced
By something much greater that cannot be defaced,
For what was "in part" has now "become whole"—
For on the "wings of the flesh," love entered the "soul"!

There's Sunshine in a Smile

Life is a mixture of sunshine and rain,
Laughter and pleasure, teardrops and pain,
All days can't be bright, but it's certainly true,
There was never a cloud the sun didn't shine through—
So just keep on smiling whatever betide you,
Secure in the knowledge God is always beside you,
And you'll find when you smile your day will be brighter
And all of your burdens will seem so much lighter—
For each time you smile you will find it is true
Somebody, somewhere will *smile back at you,*
And nothing on earth can make life more worthwhile
Than the sunshine and warmth of a *beautiful smile.*

Where There Is Love

Where there is love the heart is light,
Where there is love the day is bright,
Where there is love there is a song
To help when things are going wrong . . .
Where there is love there is a smile
To make all things seem more worthwhile,
Where there is love there's quiet peace,
A tranquil place where turmoils cease—
Love changes darkness into light
And makes the heart take "wingless flight" . . .
Oh, blest are they who walk in love,
They also walk with God above—
And when you walk with God each day
And kneel together when you pray,
Your marriage will be truly blest
And God will be your daily *"guest"*—
And love that once seemed yours alone,
God gently blends into *His Own*.

The Power of Love

There is no thinking person
   who can stand untouched today
And view the world around us
   drifting downward to decay
Without feeling deep within them
   a silent unnamed dread,
Wondering how to stem the chaos
   that lies frightfully ahead . . .
But the problems we are facing
   cannot humanly be solved
For our diplomatic strategy
   only gets us more involved
And our skillful ingenuity,
   our technology and science
Can never change a sinful heart
   filled with hatred and defiance . . .
So our problems keep on growing
   every hour of every day
As man vainly tries to solve them
   in his own *self-willful way* . . .
But man is powerless alone
   to *clean up the world outside*
Until his own polluted soul
   is *clean* and *free inside* . . .
For the amazing power of love
   is beyond all comprehension
And it alone can heal this world
   of its hatred and dissension.

What Is Love!

What is love?
    No words can define it.
It's something so great
    Only God could design it . . .
Wonder of Wonders,
    Beyond man's conception,
And only in God
    Can love find true perfection.
For love means much more
    Than small words can express,
For what man calls love
    Is so very much less
Than the beauty and depth
    And the true richness of
God's gift to mankind—
    His compassionate love . . .
For love has become
    A word that's misused,
Perverted, distorted
    And often abused . . .
To speak of "light romance"
    Or some affinity for
A passing attraction
    That is seldom much more

Than a mere interlude
    Of inflamed fascination,
A romantic fling
    Of no lasting duration . . .
But love is enduring
    And patient and kind.
It judges all things
    With the heart, not the mind.
And love can transform
    The most commonplace
Into beauty and splendor
    And sweetness and grace . . .
For love is unselfish,
    Giving more than it takes,
And no matter what happens
    Love never forsakes.
It's faithful and trusting
    And always believing,
Guileless and honest
    And never deceiving . . .
Yes, love is beyond
    What man can define,
For love is Immortal
    And God's Gift is Divine!

Strangers Are Friends We Haven't Met

God knows *no strangers,* He loves us all,
  the poor, the rich, the great, the small . . .
He is a friend who is always there
  to share our troubles and lessen our care . . .
No one is a stranger in God's sight,
  for *God is love* and in *His light*
May we, too, try in our small way
  to make *new friends* from day to day . . .
So pass no stranger with an unseeing eye,
  for God may be sending a *new friend by.*

Heart Gifts

It's not the things that can be bought
  that are life's richest treasure,
It's just the little "heart gifts"
  that money cannot measure . . .
A cheerful smile, a friendly word,
  a sympathetic nod
Are priceless little treasures
  from the storehouse of our God . . .
They are the things that can't be bought
  with silver or with gold,
For thoughtfulness and kindness
  and love are never sold . . .
They are the priceless things in life
  for which no one can pay,
And the giver finds rich recompense
  in *giving them away.*

Give Lavishly!
Live Abundantly!

The more you give, the more you get—
The more you laugh, the less you fret—
The more you do *unselfishly*,
The more you live *abundantly* . . .

The more of everything you share,
The more you'll always have to spare—
The more you love, the more you'll find
That life is good and friends are kind . . .

For only *what we give away*,
Enriches us from day to day.

The Priceless Gift

The priceless gift of life is love,
For with the help of God above
Love can change the human race
And make this world a better place—
For love dissolves all hate and fear
And makes our vision bright and clear
So we can see and rise above
Our pettiness on "wings of love."

One of the Author's Favorite Prayers

GOD, open my eyes so I may see
And feel YOUR PRESENCE close to me . . .
Give me strength for my stumbling feet
As I battle the crowd on life's busy street,
And widen the vision of my unseeing eyes
So in passing faces I'll recognize
Not just a stranger, unloved and unknown,
But a friend with a heart that is much like my own . . .
Give me perception to make me aware
That scattered profusely on life's thoroughfare
Are the best GIFTS of GOD that we daily pass by
As we look at the world with an UNSEEING EYE.

The Gift
of Friendship

Friendship is a *priceless gift* that cannot be bought or sold,
But its value is far greater than a mountain made of gold—
For gold is cold and lifeless, it can neither see nor hear,
And in the time of trouble it is powerless to cheer—
It has no ears to listen, no heart to understand,
It cannot bring you comfort or reach out a helping hand—
So when you ask God for a *gift*, be thankful if *He* sends
Not diamonds, pearls or riches, but the love of real true
    friends.

A Friend
Is a Gift of God

Among the great and glorious gifts
    our heavenly Father sends
Is the GIFT of UNDERSTANDING
    that we find in loving friends,
For in this world of trouble
    that is filled with anxious care
Everybody needs a friend
    in whom they're free to share
The little secret heartaches
    that lay heavy on their mind,
Not just a mere acquaintance
    but someone who's "JUST OUR KIND"—
For, somehow, in the generous heart
    of loving, faithful friends
The good God in His charity
    and wisdom always sends
A sense of understanding
    and the power of perception
And mixes these fine qualities
    with kindness and affection
So when we need some sympathy
    or a friendly hand to touch,
Or an ear that listens tenderly
    and speaks words that mean so much,
We seek our true and trusted friend
    in the knowledge that we'll find
A heart that's sympathetic
    and an understanding mind . . . .
And often just without a word
    there seems to be a union
Of thoughts and kindred feelings
    for GOD gives TRUE FRIENDS communion.

The Golden Chain
of Friendship

FRIENDSHIP is a GOLDEN CHAIN,
The links are friends so dear,
And like a rare and precious jewel
It's treasured more each year . . .
It's clasped together firmly
With a love that's deep and true,
And it's rich with happy memories
And fond recollections, too . . .
Time can't destroy its beauty
For, as long as memory lives,
Years can't erase the pleasure
That the joy of friendship gives . . .
For friendship is a priceless gift
That can't be bought or sold,
But to have an understanding friend
Is worth far more than gold . . .
And the GOLDEN CHAIN of FRIENDSHIP
Is a strong and blessed tie
Binding kindred hearts together
As the years go passing by.

Help Yourself to Happiness

Everybody, everywhere seeks happiness, it's true,
But finding it and keeping it seems difficult to do,
Difficult because we think that happiness is found
Only in the places where wealth and fame abound—
And so we go on searching in "palaces of pleasure"
Seeking recognition and monetary treasure,
Unaware that happiness is just a "state of mind"
Within the reach of everyone who takes time to be kind—
For in making *others happy* we will be happy, too,
For the happiness you give away returns to "shine on
  you."

A Sure Way to a Happy Day

Happiness is something we create in our mind,
It's not something you search for and so seldom find—
It's just waking up and beginning the day
By counting our blessings and kneeling to pray—
It's giving up thoughts that breed discontent
And accepting what comes as a "gift heaven-sent"—
It's giving up wishing for things we have not
And making the best of whatever we've got—
It's knowing that life is determined for us,
And pursuing our tasks without fret, fume or fuss—
For it's by completing what God gives us to do
That we find real contentment and happiness, too.

A Favorite Recipe

Take a *cup* of *Kindness*, mix it well with *Love*,
Add a lot of Patience and *Faith* in *God above*,
Sprinkle very generously with *Joy* and *Thanks* and *Cheer*—
And you'll have lots of *"Angel Food"* to feast on all the
    year.

A Thankful Heart

Take nothing for granted, for whenever you do
The "joy of enjoying" is lessened for you—
For we rob our own lives much more than we know
When we fail to respond or in any way show
Our thanks for the blessings that daily are ours . . .
The warmth of the sun, the fragrance of flowers,
The beauty of twilight, the freshness of dawn,
The coolness of dew on a green velvet lawn,
The kind little deeds so thoughtfully done,
The favors of friends and the love that someone
Unselfishly gives us in a myriad of ways,
Expecting no payment and no words of praise—
Oh, great is our loss when we no longer find
A thankful response to things of this kind,
For the *joy of enjoying* and the *Fullness of living*
Are found in the heart that is filled with *Thanksgiving*.

"Flowers Leave Their Fragrance on the Hand That Bestows Them"

There's an old Chinese proverb that, if practiced each day,
Would change the whole world in a wonderful way—
Its truth is so simple, it's so easy to do,
And it works every time and successfully, too . . .
For you can't do a kindness without a reward,
Not in silver nor gold but in joy from the Lord—
You can't light a candle to show others the way
Without feeling the warmth of that bright little ray . . .
And you can't pluck a rose, all fragrant with dew,
Without part of its fragrance remaining with you.

Make Your Day Bright by Thinking Right

Don't start your day by supposin'
    that trouble is just ahead,
It's better to stop supposin'
    and start with a prayer instead,
And make it a prayer of *thanksgiving*
    for the wonderful things God has wrought
Like the beautiful sunrise and sunset,
    "God's gifts" that are free
    and not bought—
For what is the use of supposin'
    the dire things that could happen to you
And worry about some misfortune
    that seldom if ever comes true—
But instead of just idle supposin'
    step forward to meet each new day
Secure in the knowledge God's near you
    to lead you each step of the way—
For supposin' the worst things will happen
    only helps to make them come true
And you darken the bright, happy moments
    that the dear Lord has given to you—
So if you desire to be happy
    and get rid of the *"misery of dread"*
Just give up *"supposin' the worst things"*
    and look for *"the best things"* instead.

New Beginnings

How often we wish for another chance
To make a fresh beginning,
A chance to blot out our mistakes
And change failure into winning—
And it does not take a new year
To make a brand-new start,
It only takes the deep desire
To try with all our heart
To live a little better
And to always be forgiving
And to add a little "sunshine"
To the world in which we're living—
So never give up in despair
And think that you are through,
For there's always a tomorrow
And a chance to start anew.

Give Us
Daily Awareness

On life's busy thoroughfares
We meet with angels unawares—
So, Father, make us kind and wise
So we may always recognize
The blessings that are ours to take,
The friendships that are ours to make
If we but open our heart's door wide
To let the sunshine of love inside.

"In Him We Live and Move and Have Our Being"

We walk in a world that is strange and unknown
And in the midst of the crowd we still feel alone,
We question our purpose, our part and our place
In this vast land of mystery suspended in space,
We probe and explore and try hard to explain
The tumult of thoughts that our minds entertain . . .
But all of our probings and complex explanations
Of man's inner feelings and fears and frustrations
Still leave us engulfed in the "MYSTERY of LIFE"
With all of its struggles and suffering and strife,
Unable to fathom what tomorrow will bring—
But there is one truth to which we can cling,
For while LIFE'S a MYSTERY man can't understand
The "GREAT GIVER of LIFE" is HOLDING OUR HAND
And safe in HIS care there is no need for seeing
For "IN HIM WE LIVE and MOVE and HAVE OUR
    BEING."

How Great the Yield from a Fertile Field

The farmer ploughs through the fields of green
And the blade of the plough is sharp and keen,
But the seed must be sown to bring forth grain,
For nothing is born without suffering and pain—
And God never ploughs in the soul of man
Without intention and purpose and plan,
So whenever you feel the plough's sharp blade
Let not your heart be sorely afraid
For, like the farmer, God chooses a field
From which He expects an excellent yield—
So rejoice though your heart is broken in two,
God seeks to bring forth a rich harvest in you.

On the Wings
of Prayer

Just close your eyes and open your heart
And feel your worries and cares depart,
Just yield yourself to the Father above
And let Him hold you secure in His love . . .
For life on earth grows more involved
With endless problems that can't be solved—
But God only asks us to do our best,
Then He will "take over" and finish the rest . . .
So when you are tired, discouraged and blue,
There's always one door that is open to you—
And that is the door to *"The House of Prayer"*
And you'll find God waiting to meet you there . . .
And *"The House of Prayer"* is no farther away
Than the quiet spot where you kneel and pray—
For the heart is a temple when God is there
As we place ourselves in His loving care.
And He hears every prayer and answers each one
When we pray in His name *"Thy will be done"*—
And the burdens that seemed too heavy to bear
Are lifted away on *"the wings of prayer."*

Thank God for Little Things

Thank You, God, for little things
    that often come our way—
The things we take for granted
    but don't mention when we pray—
The unexpected courtesy,
    the thoughtful, kindly deed—
A hand reached out to help us
    in the time of sudden need—

Oh make us more aware, dear God,
    of little daily graces
That come to us with "sweet surprise"
    from never-dreamed-of places.

My God Is No Stranger

I've never seen God, but I know how I feel . . .
It's people like *you* who make *Him* "so real" . . .
My God is no stranger, *He's* friendly and gay . . .
And *He* doesn't ask me to weep when I pray . . .
It seems that I pass *Him* so often each day . . .
In the faces of people I meet on my way . . .
He's the stars in the heaven, a smile on some face . . .
A leaf on a tree or a rose in a vase . . .
He's winter and autumn and summer and spring . . .
In short, *God Is Every Real, Wonderful Thing* . . .
I wish I might meet *Him* much more than I do . . .
I would if there were *more people like you.*

Beyond Our Asking

More than hearts can imagine or minds comprehend,
God's bountiful gifts are ours without end—
We ask for a cupful when the vast sea is ours,
We pick a small rosebud from a garden of flowers,
We reach for a sunbeam but the sun still abides,
We draw one short breath but there's air on all sides—
Whatever we ask for falls short of God's giving
For *His greatness* exceeds every facet of living,
And always God's ready and eager and willing
To pour out His mercy completely fulfilling
All of man's needs for peace, joy and rest
For God gives His children *whatever is best*—
Just give Him a chance to open *His treasures*
And He'll fill your life with unfathomable pleasures,
Pleasures that never grow worn-out and faded
And leave us depleted, disillusioned and jaded—
For God has a "storehouse" just filled to the brim
With all that man needs if we'll only ask Him.

He Loves You!

It's amazing and incredible,
But it's as true as it can be,
God loves and understands us all
And that means *you* and *me*—
His grace is all sufficient
For both the *young* and *old*,
For the lonely and the timid,
For the brash and for the bold—
His love knows no exceptions,
So never feel excluded
No matter *who* or *what* you are
Your name has been included—
And no matter what your past has been,
Trust God to understand,
And no matter what your problem is
Just place it in His Hand—
For in all of our *unloveliness*
This *Great God loves us still,*
He loved us since the world began
And what's more, *He always will!*

Fulfillment

Apple blossoms bursting wide
    now beautify the tree
And make a Springtime picture
    that is beautiful to see . . .
Oh, fragrant lovely blossoms,
    you'll make a bright bouquet
If I but break your branches
    from the apple tree today . . .
But if I break your branches
    and make your beauty mine,
You'll bear no fruit in season
    when severed from the vine . . .
And when we cut ourselves away
    from guidance that's divine,
Our lives will be as fruitless
    as the branch without the vine . . .
For as the flowering branches
    depend upon the tree
To nourish and fulfill them
    till they reach futurity,
We too must be dependent
    on our Father up above,
For we are but the *branches*
    and He's *the tree of love.*

Never Borrow Sorrow from Tomorrow

Deal only with the present,
Never step into tomorrow,
For God asks us just to trust Him
And to never borrow sorrow—
For the future is not ours to know
And it may never be,
So let us live and give our best
And give it lavishly—
For to meet tomorrow's troubles
Before they are even ours
Is to anticipate the Saviour
And to doubt His all-wise powers—
So let us be content to solve
Our problems one by one,
Asking nothing of tomorrow
Except "*Thy Will be done.*"

God Knows Best

Our Father knows what's best for us,
So why should we complain—
We always want the sunshine,
But He knows there must be rain—
We love the sound of laughter
And the merriment of cheer,
But our hearts would lose their tenderness
If we never shed a tear . . .
Our Father tests us often
With suffering and with sorrow,
He tests us, not to punish us,
But to help us meet *tomorrow* . . .
For growing trees are strenghtened
When they withstand the storm,
And the sharp cut of the chisel
Gives the marble grace and form . . .
God never hurts us needlessly,
And He never wastes our pain,
For every loss He sends to us
Is followed by rich gain . . .
And when we count the blessings
That God has so freely sent,
We will find no cause for murmuring
And no time to lament . . .
For Our Father loves His children,
And to Him all things are plain,
So He never sends us *pleasure*
When the *soul's deep need is pain* . . .
So whenever we are troubled,
And when everything goes wrong,
It is just God working in us
To make *our spirit strong.*

Things
to Be Thankful For

The good, green earth beneath our feet,
The air we breathe, the food we eat,
Some work to do, a goal to win,
A hidden longing deep within
That spurs us on to bigger things
And helps us meet what each day brings,
All these things and many more
Are things we should be thankful for . . .
And most of all our thankful prayers
Should rise to God because He cares!

"The Fruit of the Spirit Is Love and Peace"

There is no thinking person
Who can stand untouched today
And view the world around us
Slowly drifting to decay
Without feeling deep within him
A silent, unnamed dread
As he contemplates the future
That lies frighteningly ahead . . .
For, like watching storm clouds gather
In a dark and threatening sky,
Man knows that there is nothing
He can formulate or try
That will stop the storm from breaking
In its fury and its force,
Nor can he change or alter
The storm's destructive course,
But his anxious fears are lessened
When he calls on God above,
For he knows above the storm clouds
Is the brightness of God's love . . .
So as the *"clouds of chaos"*

Gather in man's muddled mind,
And he searches for the answer
He *alone* can never find,
Let us recognize we're facing
Problems man has never solved,
And with all our daily efforts
Life grows more and more involved,
But our future will seem brighter
And we'll meet with less resistance
If we call upon our Father
And seek Divine Assistance . . .
For the spirit can unravel
Many tangled, knotted threads
That defy the skill and power
Of the world's best hands and heads,
And our plans for growth and progress,
Of which we all have dreamed,
Cannot survive materially
Unless *our spirits* are redeemed . . .
And only through a living *faith*
Can man achieve this goal,
For safety and security
Are born within the soul.

The Answer

In the tiny petal
    of a tiny flower
        that grew from a tiny pod . . .
Is the *miracle*
    and the *mystery*
        of *all creation* and *God!*